YOUTUBE

Top 10 Strategies to Create a
Successful YouTube Channel and
Make Money Online (YouTube
Channel Guide to Grow Passive
Income through Social Media)

By JOSHUA ELANS

Table of Contents

Introduction

Are you tired of working your nine to five job wondering when you're going to make enough money to retire or, at least, take that vacation you've been planning?

Would you like to know how to make money without having to constantly manage the source?

Then you should look into YouTube videos! There are plenty of ways you can monetize your YouTube videos and create ones that will be successful. In this book, you'll learn the top ten ways to make money on YouTube.

You'll learn how to:

- Generate Traffic to Your Blog Or Website via YouTube Videos
- Make Products and Promote them with YouTube
- Generate Affiliate Sales from YouTube
- Make a Web TV Series
- Become a YouTube Personality or Star
- Use the YouTube Partner Program
- Make Tutorial Videos
- Boost Your Fundraising Campaign's Results
- Build Your Brand
- Turn Your Pet or Child into a Star

You'll also learn how to optimize your YouTube video's SEO as an added bonus at the end of this book!

YouTube videos are an excellent way to make an extra, passive income. All you have to do is make some videos, optimize them with SEO, and watch the viewers pile up!

If you're ready to learn how to make your YouTube videos generate income for you, then scroll down and grab a copy of this book today!

Chapter One – Using YouTube for Traffic

If you have a website or a blog, then using YouTube to get traffic to it is a wonderful idea! Many websites were hard hit when Google updated their SEO programs, and if you're one of those people, then you're most likely hurting right now. You can use YouTube to not only regain traffic but to also gain *more* traffic than you had before!

There are a few different ways you can do this.

Repurpose Content

The easiest way to make videos that pertain to your blog is to go back through some old blog posts and repurpose them into videos. For example, if you have a cooking blog set up a decent camera and film yourself making one of your popular recipes. You can then put that video on YouTube, link it back to your blog, and watch the viewers roll in!

Once you have your content repurposed or you've made some new videos with fresh content, take a look at the tips below.

Tip #1: Tell Them What To Do

This is the easiest step for all bloggers and YouTubers out there, but it's also one of the most overlooked steps. At the end of every video, you have to specifically communicate a compelling call to action and inform people on how to get to your website and *why* they should get to your website!

This step can be done with one very simple line. It can be something such as:

Thank you for watching today! To discover the top ten ways to make money on YouTube, head over to my website (insert website) and look into what made me such a successful YouTuber!

When you tell people what to do and why they need to do it, they will take action with you.

Tip #2: The Video Description Box

Every time you go to upload a video on YouTube, there is a video description box that you should never fail to fill in! Most marketers don't bother taking advantage of this function, but if you do, you'll see a boost in blog traffic in no time!

To turn the video description box into a traffic-generating machine here's all you have to do. Just add five to six call to action words at the beginning with a complete website URL. It can be something like this:

Make money with YouTube: (insert URL)

The URL becomes a clickable link that any viewer will be able to see under the video. While this is an excellent start, you should probably add a few paragraphs to describe what's in your video. That way you can add the website URL again at the end of the description.

Tip #3: The Overlay of Your Call to Action

The third and last way to convert a video viewer into a highly-targeted traffic blow viewer is through a feature known as Call-To-Action Overlay. An overlay is just a little banner ad that will sit on the lower third of the video. You have control over the thumbnail image, words, and the destination where you want to send the viewers.

This function is just a few minutes to set up, but failing to add it to your videos will cause you to miss a lot of traffic.

In order to begin this feature, you have to start by signing up for ad.YouTube.com.

Once you have viewers to a blog that makes money, you'll make even more money with the increase in traffic!

Chapter Two – Make Products and Promote Them on YouTube

If you're making your own products or you'd like to start creating them, then YouTube offers many different ways you can promote a product and make a sale. You can promote products such as apps, eBooks, art, and even music. Make a product, add it to a shopping cart, and then use your YouTube channel to promote them. Just be sure you put a link to your product in your video's description so viewers can purchase it! Just take a look at a few different examples of how to promote products on YouTube below.

Promoting eBooks

Promoting a book on YouTube is as easy as making a short video yourself about the topic, whether it's non-fiction or fiction, or making a video about *why* you wrote about that topic. You can also hire a professional videographer off many different freelance websites in order to get a professionally made video that really speaks to what your book is about. Just make sure you put a link to the book in the description and have a call to action at the end!

Promoting Music

You don't have to have a video of the music in order to promote your music unless you want to. You could make a video explaining what all your songs are about and why they are important. Do an interview video where you have someone ask you questions, and make it interesting!

Of course, you could do the tried but true method of making a video that correlates with your song. Then put the link to iTunes or any other site where you sell your music so they can go buy it!

Promoting Products

If you're an inventor and you've made a product or you've had one made for you that you rebranded, promoting it on YouTube is essential! Make videos of yourself using the product, talk about its benefits, and most importantly, talk about why people need to buy your product! How is it going to make their lives easier or happier? Why should they spend their money on your product and not someone else's product?

Tying It All Together

YouTube is not just for YouTube viewers. You can post links on your professional website and post links to social media that potential customers to your video. Be sure you promote your video using different outlets other than YouTube!

Chapter Three – Affiliate Sales on YouTube

Affiliate marketing is selling a product in exchange for a commission. It's a lot like being a real estate agent except you're selling someone else's product online. There are thousands of companies that offer up very striking deals to affiliate marketers who promote products and end up causing a sale. Some of these companies are Amazon and eBay. There are also affiliate networks available for you to join, such as Commission Junction and ClickBank.

To make money off YouTube as an affiliate marketer you can try out these tips.

#1: Review Videos

The most popular option for obtaining affiliate sales via YouTube is to create videos that review the products. Make a video of yourself or someone else using the product or talking about the benefits of using the product. If you like to sell makeup items, make some videos with tutorials on how to apply the makeup. If you're someone who is selling woodworking products, then make a video on how to use it in an everyday project!

#2: Link Backs

Be sure you include an affiliate link in your description and at least once in the video so that people will purchase the product via your affiliate account. You don't want them to watch your video, go to Amazon or eBay themselves, and then purchase the product without going through your link!

#3: Don't Forget SEO!

Search engine optimization is just as important with a video as it is with a blog post! Be sure you put SEO terms in your description and in your tag sections. These are important for getting your target audience to your video. If you don't' utilize SEO, chances are you won't be seen.

#4 How-To Videos

You don't need to mention the product directly in the video like a review video. You can make a video that includes the item you're trying to sell without actually making it completely about the item.

Chapter Four – Create a Web TV Series

Do you like telling stories or acting? Then you can create a web TV series on YouTube. You're only limited by your imagination and your budget, but mostly your imagination. You could make a comedy series, a talk show, or a drama series. Be aware that YouTube will limit your video length to fifteen minutes. To upload a longer video, you need to increase the limit. If you're a frustrated screenwriter, then get some friends together and record a TV series. You never know, if you get a lot of reviews, you might take this to an entirely different level! Take a look at some things you need to consider when creating a YouTube web TV series.

#1: Audience

It seems simple and redundant considering most people tell you to think about audience, but it's imperative you think about them and have one if you create any type of series for people to view. Making a strong intention of who the intended audience is for your series will save you a lot of time and frustration later on down the line. Obviously, asking yourself this question not new to the entire storytelling process. Having a clear vision of your target audience alleviates any stress down the line when it comes time to promote that series.

#2: Your Calling Card or For the Fans?

Are you making these videos with industry consideration in mind or are you planning to make a creative at-home movie? Figure out where you want to end up with this. Do you want to become famous and be able to command a television presence, too, or do you want to focus on making money only on YouTube?

#3: Cast the Right Actors

You not only want people who are right for the role, but you want those who will attract viewers. Grow your YouTube profile and start becoming friends with some of the big name people on there. They are looking for ways they can grow their market and their audience, and you *need* an audience. See if the two of you can't work together and cast them in some of your films.

#4: Ancillary Content

Millennials, the ones who are most likely going to view your content on YouTube, want to see the actors who are behind the characters in the series. So be sure you have some sneak peeks to what happens when you make an episode. Break down that fourth wall and let them in so that they can feel connected with the actors. This helps build the brand!

#5: Plan the Series

You shouldn't just plan the season when you're making a YouTube series. Plan out the entire series and have a basic idea of where it's going to go. You don't have to have all the details, but knowing where the entire series is going to end up is a good idea. You don't want to get stuck on the drawing board when you should beginning season two if you've had an amazing season one!

#6: Allot for Marketing Budget

Most people make the mistake of spending all their money on hiring actors, paying for props, and purchasing an expensive camera, but you need money for marketing, too! If you don't advertise your video, chances are you will not be found and become a YouTube hit.

#7: Do Your Research

Educate yourself about the best structures for YouTube videos. If you don't know what's already working, you can't tweak it to turn it into a huge moneymaker for you! So educate yourself on the best practices of creating a YouTube video and go from there.

Chapter Five: Become a YouTube Personality

YouTube stars make a decent amount of money every year. Some of them are millionaires! For example, BlueXephos has almost a billion channel views. Considering most YouTubers make about seven dollars per one thousand views, that's almost seven million dollars so far! Take a look at what some famous YouTube stars say you should do if you want to become a YouTube Star.

#1: Don't Follow Trends

A lot of people who want to become YouTube stars will look at what's popular on YouTube right now and then they copy it. There's a much better starting point based on what people are not watching!

Ask yourself what is missing from YouTube right now and what you'd like to see on there. A lot of people concentrate on what people are watching at the moment, but that's not the best way to go. Someone has already done that. You need to find something they haven't done yet.

#2: Be Patient

It takes a while to become a massive success on YouTube. Be patient and keep making videos as you wait for that first one to take off. Once the right crowd shares your videos and they are seen by hundreds of others, they will then go back and view the old videos, so it's better to have a surplus of videos.

#3: Invest in Equipment

If you have a decent Smartphone in your pocket, then you might already be set to get started on YouTube! All you need is a little tripod to attach it to and you can get filming. If you have steady hands, you might not even need that. Once you start making money with those videos, invest in a decent camera and you can make even better videos! It's not that expensive to purchase filming equipment, and you can always look for some decent used ones on eBay or another site like it.

#4: You Don't Need A Large Crew

If you have a significant other or just a friend who wants to help out, that's really all you need in the beginning. Have them hold the camera for you and help you out with the makeup and accounting. It's really great that you get to wear a bunch of different hats in your company rather than relying on others. If you get larger and you feel the need to hire a crew, then keep it small. You don't want to get too large too fast and end up being just another YouTube sensation that's gone in fifteen minutes.

#5: Invest In Social Media

YouTubers do not just interact with their fans on the main site, YouTube, they also interact with their fans on sites like Twitter, Facebook, Pinterest, and much more. It's an important part of the job. In fact, it's almost as important as making the video in the first place. Without the fans and without the interaction with the fans, you won't create more fans or hold their interest. They want to know that you care they're watching your videos, so show them!

#6: Collaborate Smartly

Collaboration is one of the best ways you can build your YouTube channel audience. But it's not enough that you want to collaborate. You should also think about what you have that's original that you bring to the table. You should be interacting and making a video with someone else rather than just sitting in or whatever it is they do. Bring some animation or music skills to the table, or have an interesting location where the two of you can film.

E-mail is probably not the best way to collaborate because they can get lost easily. While it might seem odd, asking for someone's phone number if you're serious about collaborating is not uncommon. Speaking on the phone or through Skype is much easier than trying to keep track of e-mails.

#7: Consider Multiple Channels

All YouTubers start off with just one channel, but as you get more popular, you should launch a few others to avoid the one-size-fits-all approach. Depending on your target audience, there might be some different things you want to say or do in order to attract them to your videos. For example, you need to use different dialogue for teenagers while you should use something completely different for adults.

Chapter Six – Utilizing the YouTube Partner Program

Once you've made several videos, it's about time you joined the YouTube Partner Program. All you have to do is enable your videos for monetization. You then receive a share of the income from advertising. Just as YouTube stars do, you'll be paid for every one thousand views you get on a video.

Here are a few tips to getting started with monetization.

#1: Enable Monetization

In order to monetize a video so that an ad shows up before the video plays, you have to first enable it. This means you are allowing YouTube to put ads on the videos and that you legally agree there isn't any copyright content in the video other than your own.

You can monetize manually through checking the Monetize with Ads box in the monetization tab during the uploading process. If you want to perform this for a video that's already been uploaded, then you just have to go to the video manager and click the dollar sign symbol next to the video you'd like to monetize.

#2: Build Traffic

It's always a good idea to build some traffic before you monetize a video. That's because it just so happens that users viewing a video for the first time are annoyed by the ads and they leave. Therefore, keep in mind that you want to build a good audience for the channel before you begin adding monetization. Have a few ad-free videos so that you retain the audience in the form of subscribers.

Chapter Seven – Make Tutorial Videos

Tutorial videos are very popular on YouTube. If you know how to do something well and you're able to teach others, then you can make money from your videos. While beauty videos are popular at the moment, you should do what you feel most comfortable with. However, you can't just make a video showing yourself doing something. You have to have a format to make it a teachable video, so let's go over a good format.

Step One: Planning

The first step is to plan your video. Behind any good instructional video, there is a plan that outlines the content you'll be covering. Here are the important elements you want to consider in your plan before you begin filming:

- **Learning goals.** What do you want your viewers to gain knowledge-wise?
- **Course outline.** Create a list of the topics you'll be covering.
- **Target video length.** With today's tight schedules, a bite-sized video is much better. Consider breaking it up into seven-minute chapters for easy viewing.
- **Subject matter expert.** Find someone you know who has extensive knowledge about your topic. You need

someone who can assist you with the planning process and help you with the content. They can even spend some time in front of the camera!

- **Date.** Select a date and time for the practice run and video shoot.

- **Location.** Choose an appropriate location for the shoot.

- **Budget.** You need a budget for the crew and the video. Keep in mind that a good instructional video just needs good subject matter and a camera operator.

Step Two: The Basics

You need to understand the basics of an instructional video. Begin the video by introducing whose speaking and outlining what's going to be covered in the course. Present the material and wrap up the video with a summary of what the viewer saw. The other important element to think about is an association to the student. If you're demonstrating some software, spread screen shots with some face time to keep the listeners interested.

Step Three: Pre-production and Practice

Go through the outline of the course with your expert ahead of time so there is time for fine-tuning. The more comfortable the presenter is on screen, the more engaged the viewers are going to be. Some subject matter experts like to use cue cards to increase their comfort level, so be sure to establish that on the day of the shoot. Allow their personality to shine, and don't worry about going to for perfection.

Step Four: Shoot

Focus on making the expert feel comfortable in front of the camera. Break the film up into short segments to help with this situation. Keep the process fun and simple, and the results will speak volumes.

Step Five: Post-Production

Review the video and then edit it when necessary. Consider adding some closed captions to the video. This helps disabled viewers, and it also helps optimize your Google search results.

Step Six: Online Learner's Experience

If you're making the video for the web, you might want to compress the video depending on the bandwidth the viewer has. To keep it simple, make videos H264 or FLV that use a Flash 9 or greater. The greatest way to make sure everybody is able to view your videos is to use a content delivery network to host them, such as YouTube.

Chapter Eight – Boost Fundraising Results

YouTube is a great resource for market research. You can soon discover if your brilliant idea or your new book is going to make money or not. If you've recently developed an idea for a product but you need some funding, make some videos before you create a Kickstarter campaign. The views and the comments on the video will tell you whether the idea is viable. The audience can even help you make it viable, so your efforts to be funded are successful.

#1 Reaction

You first need to decide how you want your audience to react to the video emotionally. Mold the video around that goal because feelings are what inspire people to contribute. Here are few examples.

If you want a viewer to feel compassion, a profile of the problem will be a huge benefit, or use some statistics to show the scope of the problem.

To bring about nostalgia, you can use someone else's recollections to trigger the viewer's memories.

#2 Focus on a Story or Detail

Don't try to show every part of an organization or a project because most of the viewers are not going to be interested. Focus on what the product will do to change lives rather than the nitty-gritty details of what it does.

#3 Avoid Clichés

Never say things like 'for the price of a cup of coffee every day' or 'making the world a better place.' They don't work because people have learned to ignore them.

#4 Tell Them How To Help

Tell your audience exactly how they can take action and help you achieve the goal of raising money. Whether this is for a product or a fundraising campaign for a non-profit, tell them where they can find more information about what they're donating to and how they can donate.

#5 Get Feedback

Find people who are not involved in the cause and get feedback from them. Ask them whether the video comes across in a positive way, is coherent, and if it's interesting to an outsider.

Once you've done all that, upload the video to YouTube and don't forget to have it on your campaign, too!

Chapter Nine – Build Your Brand

You're a brand and you have power. Utilizing YouTube allows you to amplify you no matter what you're doing, what your job is, YouTube can help you be known for your strengths and help you make money. Even if you don't have a clear idea of how you can make money on YouTube get started with videos of your passions and interest. You might just stumble across a goldmine, just as those who have filmed their pets have.

Here are some ideas to get you started.

#1: Hobbyist Videos

If you have a hobby, then film yourself doing it and make it into an instructional video! For example, let's say you like model trains. Film your collection and have a separate video on each type of train. Film a video that shows how to create the layout of the terrain for your train and how to put the tracks together. Every aspect of your model train hobby is a potential video waiting to happen!

#2: Career Videos

If you have a career where you think there might be teachable moments, like a plumber knowing how to fix a leaky pipe, profit from that knowledge! Use your expert knowledge to make a video of whatever it is you do for a living and teach people how to do it or why they should be doing it.

#3: Instructional Videos

You might think this goes along with career videos, but what about women who know how to do their makeup just right? It's not really a hobby and it's not really a career unless you're a makeup artist, so where does it fit? It's just something you know how to do well. Figure out something like that and make some tutorials on it!

Chapter Ten – Turn Your Pet or Child into a Star

Just about everyone has heard of Grumpy Cat. She's a worldwide star with photo shoots and commercial campaigns now. You don't have to be a singer to become a star on YouTube. If you're lucky, you can shoot a video of a child, pet, or a double rainbow that looks really neat and you'll become a YouTube star.

So keep the camera ready for anything you can take a video of, especially if it involves children or pets, and get ready to hit that play button. You might just catch something on camera that becomes the next worldwide sensation!

However, if you want to leave it more to skill than chance, you might want to read the next section on SEO optimization for your YouTube videos. All the aforementioned techniques will benefit from optimizing your SEO.

Conclusion

Search engine optimization is the most important part of your video, other than the video itself. Without it, you won't get views. If you don't add tags, descriptions, and many other elements to your videos, you'll be wasting your time. So here are the ways you can optimize your SEO for YouTube videos.

Video Descriptions

You have to remember that YouTube is not able to watch or listen to the video yet, and neither is Google. That means you have to rely heavily on the text that surrounds your video to understand the video's topic. If you have a description with just a sentence, you're not going to get a lot of views. The more YouTube knows about the video from the description, the better it will be able to rank it for your target audience. Your video descriptions should be at least two hundred words.

Video Keyword Optimization

Ranking on YouTube is wonderful, but ranking on both YouTube and Google at the same time is a lot better. While Google gives YouTube videos an edge in the search engine result pages, that's only true for specific keywords. These are known as video keywords because they tend to have video results on the first page of Google. For example, the keyword cute cats will always have video results.

This makes a lot of sense if you think about it. Someone searching for cute puppies or cute kittens isn't going to want an article that talks about the ten reasons cats are so cute or why puppies are adorable. However, someone who is searching for ankle sprain probably wants to see articles about symptoms and treatments. Google understands this and will show text results before they show video results.

So the bottom line is because you decide on the keywords for your video, check to see if Google has video results on the first page for that word. If they do, then it's one you should greatly contemplate because you could become the next video on Google, then.

Online Communities

You can get more video views from online communities such as Quora or LinkedIn groups. These are great places to funnel some traffic to your YouTube channel and videos. However, most communities don't like it if someone drops links to content all over the place. But they're usually open to someone sharing some helpful videos that pertain to the information.

Due to the number and quality of the video views you have playing a factor in your YouTube ranking, getting views from your target audience will work better than random people. Just find a question in the online forum that your video might help answer. Then provide some insight into the situation and suggest people watch your video if they'd like more information.

Encourage Linking and Subscribing

Due to YouTube's algorithm not using backlinks, it puts a lot of emphasis on user experience signals. If people like watching your video, expect it to jump to the top of the YouTube charts immediately. Liking and subscribing are two of the most important signals that YouTube takes into consideration. When someone likes a video enough that they subscribe after they see it, it sends a strong message to YouTube that you have a really great video.

Likes are less important but they do still count. If you want to increase the amount of likes you have and subscribers you have, then just ask people! At the end of the video, give a strong call to action that encourages them to subscribe.

Create a Keyword Rich Playlist

Never leave your YouTube channel a mess. One of the easiest ways to get more traffic to your videos is to organize your videos into a playlist. A keyword-laden playlist gives YouTube more information about the video's topic. More text-based content means you get more views.

And that's how you get more viewers to your channels and videos! Just make sure you have relevant keywords that pertain to the content in your videos, and you'll get viewers.

Thank you for reading this book about how to make money on YouTube!

www.ingramcontent.com/pod-product-compliance
Lightning Source LLC
Chambersburg PA
CBHW070424190526
45169CB00003B/1395